MW00614070

ISBN 978-0-9914952-1-4
Printed in the USA

For more information visit:
WorryWoos.com

HELPING YOUNG CHILDREN
MANAGE FRUSTRATION & ANGER

A PRACTICAL GUIDE FOR PARENTS AND
EDUCATORS TO HELP THEIR LITTLE TWITCHES!

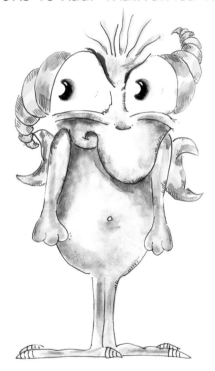

By Dr. John Irvine, PhD • Illustrated by Andi Green

Foundation booklet for The WorryWoo Monster series and companion
manual to *The Very Frustrated Monster* by Andi Green

Table of Contents:

Recently, I met with a group of moms whose kids all seemed to have some form of anger management issue. We had just read Andi Green's book *The Very Frustrated Monster* and were having a bit of a chuckle. You'd have to laugh—or you'd cry—about all the dilemmas Twitch, the main character, faced that upset him so much! Every parent was in agreement, nodding and saying how much Twitch was like her own child who had one or all of the following characteristics:

☑ Has difficulty staying calm

☑ Is easily angered

☑ Has difficulty getting over anger

☑ Says that no-one understands him

☑ Claims that no-one listens to her

☑ Feels he can't control his emotions

What they discussed was not that unusual; however, after that exchange, things became quite interesting! It came out that, while all the kids resembled Twitch in some ways, they still demonstrated an array of differences. Within that one twitchy character, the moms identified many variations.

One very chatty parent said her Twitch never stopped, never listened, got over-excited, and exploded in anger.

Another chimed in that her child wasn't hyperactive but would have a meltdown if he didn't get his way.

One fashionably dressed lady said her child was nothing like the above two but was so competitive that any failure would cause a volcanic eruption.

One exasperated mom wondered why her Twitch was an absolute "angel" outdoors and at school, but an angry, defiant "devil" at home.

One said that her son was so self-centered that everything had to be his way or the highway; she said his meltdowns were horrific!

Finally, a more quiet and retiring mom said her daughter was down on herself, super self-critical, and always angry, because she felt that she "wasn't good enough."

As the stories were shared, the parents came to realize that, although their Twitches might demonstrate some of the same frustrations and anger, we had actually identified at least six different profiles! This book evolved as I tried to help families cope with their little Twitches. Although we can't do much about the frustration that triggers each reaction, we can learn to manage the angry feelings behind each aggressive response and in turn defuse what could become an unsettling situation.

I'd like you to rate your child, whom I'll call "Twitch," on the symptoms listed below for each of the six types. On the line provided next to a descriptive phrase, place a 0—if the descriptor is never true, 1—if sometimes true, and a 2—always true.

Once you have completed this task, you may notice that the answers are scattered with 1s and 2s. That's OK, but you may also find that maybe one or more of the sections have all 2s! If that's the case, then that defines your biggest area(s) of challenge.

Now, I know we could give formal psychological labels to each type, but labels aren't the point of this book. However, if you are concerned about your child's profile and want a formal diagnosis, then visit a well-respected local clinical child psychologist.

Now, let's look at the separate profiles:

1. HYPER REACTIVE TWITCH (HT) _____

- Demands that his needs be met NOW
- Is extremely active and reactive, noisy and always on the go
- Never listens to reason
- Is emotionally volatile and overreacts BIG TIME

2. IRRITABLE TWITCH (IT) _____

- Is very critical of her own mistakes
- Says she is not good at anything
- Is chronically irritable, cries easily, and scowls constantly
- Throws long and intense temper tantrums

3. VOLCANIC TWITCH (VT) ——————

- Is very competitive
- Explodes if emotionally "overloaded"
- Becomes devastated if defeated in a game or found to have made a mistake
- Sets unreasonably high performance goals

4. ENTITLED TWITCH (ET) ——————

- Must have things his way
- Is unreasonably demanding of others
- Has a meltdown if he's told no
- Constantly battles against boundaries

5. SELF-FOCUSED/BLINKERED TWITCH (ST) ——————

- Is distressed by any changes
- Sees things as either black or white; will not compromise
- Can only see things from her viewpoint, like a blinkered horse that can only see in one direction
- Always blames someone else when something goes wrong

6. OPPOSITIONAL TWITCH (OT) ——————

- Is selectively defiant (e.g., great kid at school or with grandparents, but angry and defiant at home in general or specifically when interacting with one particular parent)
- As a general pattern, responds to domestic requests with opposition and anger
- Doesn't care about punishment or consequences
- Argues with a specific adult or adults (typically one or both parents)

BUT WHY IS MY TWITCH SO ANGRY?

OK, so you know which Twitch is your Twitch, but that doesn't explain WHY your child is easily angered or frustrated. Here's where many caring parents will go down the guilt path, blaming themselves for causing the problem behavior(s)! But, if that was the case, then other kids in the family would have the same profile.

What I've done below is to isolate possible causes so we can see what might be having the most impact in your child's life. Once we've worked out what's having an impact, we can see what changes could be made to reduce your child's frustration and anger.

Of course, research has shown that genes play a huge part, but so can the child's thinking style and place in the family, the family's social setting and lifestyle, and parent role modelling and management style. Let's look at these factors.

Personal, Family, and Societal Issues

Directions:

The following lines represent extremes. Place an X in between the two extremes that would roughly represent where your child's behavior or habits fall on that issue. **There is no scoring.** The exercise is just a way to get a feel for the factors that may be playing a part in your child's difficulties.

Physical/biological issues

Has a healthy diet _____	Has a poor diet/eats junk food
Goes to sleep easily _____	Is a poor, restless sleeper
Is motivated to exercise _____	Prefers to be sedentary
Has low/no food intolerances _____	Has severe food intolerances
Has a placid disposition _____	Is volatile and moody
Is affectionate _____	Is detached

Psychological issues

Is optimistic	Is pessimistic
Is a good problem solver	Is overwhelmed by problems
Has a patient style	Is very impatient
Shows good frustration tolerance	Shows low frustration tolerance
Is cooperative	Is defiant and oppositional

Sibling issues

Shares parental attention	Demands excessive parental attention
Has a reasonable relationship with sibling(s)	Has a friction-filled relationship with sibling(s)
Has a sibling(s) who is a good role model	Has a sibling(s) who is a poor frustration manager
Has a healthy sibling(s)	Has a sibling(s) with special needs or a demanding sibling(s)

Wider social issues

Makes friends easily	Experiences lots of peer friction
Is popular	Is rejected or a loner
Has a good relationship with extended family	Has a poor or no relationship with extended family
Likes the teacher/caregiver	Has a poor relationship with the teacher/caregiver

Parents as Role Models and Behavior Managers

How we handle our own frustrations plays a huge part in our children's behavior and attitudes.

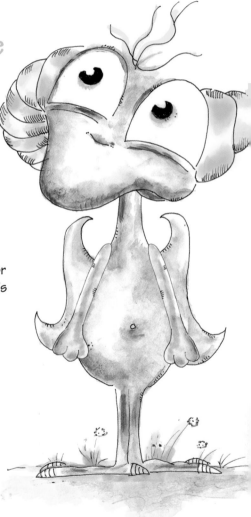

Kids copy! And, in case you think we can mask our true feelings, the fact is most of what we communicate to our children is through **tone and body language**, rather than the words we use.

In the next exercise, place an X where you would rate your own performance as a role model and child behavior manager. If two partners are actively involved in Twitch's life, you might like to use a different colored X to indicate the other rater.

As role models, we...

use positive self-talk	use negative self-talk
are good problem solvers	are stress merchants
enjoy other adults	have few adult friends
show good frustration tolerance	show low frustration tolerance
are patient	are impatient
have high self-esteem	have low self-esteem
have a reasonable marital relationship	have a friction-filled marital relationship
exercise or play a sport regularly	have little exercise
have a good work-life balance	are workaholics

As behavior managers, we...

encourage good behavior	discourage bad behavior
say yes more often than no	say no more often than yes
don't waiver—no means no	waiver—no is half hearted
have clear, consistent rules	tend to be very inconsistent
can use humor to defuse conflict	maintain angry confrontation
can state desired behavior	rely on smacking undesired behavior

If BOTH parents rated these dimensions, you may find that your ratings are often miles apart. Keep in mind that there's some truth to the old saying that opposites attract. But what I'm hoping is that, by the end of the book, when you review your ratings, you will see that many of the factors that can be changed have travelled left toward the "preferred" end of the line. And I'm hoping that the responses between parents on their self-ratings are also more closely aligned.

It's all very well knowing why Twitch may be behaving badly, but let's look at where we can start to help. And that starts with a bit of a check-up:

☐ Do a medical check. There could be many biochemical reasons that are irritating a child's little system. As mentioned above, these could relate to food, brain chemistry, or neurological factors. Some parents and experts also believe that certain chemicals in our food can make kids feel restless and angry. Foods and additives such as soda, sauce, sugar, preservatives, colorings, flavorings, and yeast have often been named as culprits.

☐ Do a marital check. If parents are at war, even if it's a stalemate, Twitch will soak up the scene and act out his confusion accordingly. Relationship counselling is something every couple needs from time to time.

☐ Do a self-check. Again, I stress that chronic or explosive anger and irritability in either mother OR father will not only be copied by the kids but will add to the child's coping difficulties. It is absolutely vital that parents role model appropriate responses to difficult emotions if they want their kids to learn to control their own anger.

☐ Do a child perspective check. Your Twitch may well feel that she has to always be the best at something to get your approval, or that another sibling is loved more, or that you're just "too busy."

☐ Do a behavior management check. If the family's method of managing a behavioral problem or frustration is violent, then the kids will copy! What we're after is a balance of soft love and firm love: tenderness blended with a no-nonsense approach (see ideas below).

☐ Do an environmental check. Is your Twitch showing the same behaviors at school, at grandma's house, and at auntie's place? If problem behaviors are displayed at some places and not others, then that tells us heaps. But also check your own domestic environment (see top tips below). If there's a lot of stress and aggression going on around Twitch, then you can bet he'll react and copy this behavior. The school environment also plays a big part in our kids' lives. If the angry behavior is new and uncharacteristic, then problems with bullying, or with the teacher, or with the school work could well be worth checking out.

Top 10 Domestic Environment Triggers for Twitch's Behavior

1. The parents are at war (whether they're separated or living together).

2. Friends or other family members are modelling angry and aggressive interactions.

3. Parents have a chaotic parenting style; their management style is unpredictable and inconsistent.

4. There is a favored sibling or a sibling with a disability and/or chronic illness.

5. The children have a poor eating regimen, including low water intake or eating/drinking lots of sugars, starches, junk food, processed food, etc.

6. The kids spend excessive amounts of time (more than 2 hours per day) on screen time—iPhones, Video Games, iPads, iPods, TV, etc.

7. The family lifestyle is too hectic; parents are too busy to connect.

8. The parent(s) is too self-absorbed or preoccupied with his or her own needs to notice the overload warning signs in the child.

9. The parents manage the children's behavior by yelling or by physical punishment.

10. There are some bullying, cyber bullying, and/or peer problems at school that impact the child's behavior at home.

OK, WE NOW KNOW WHAT MAY BE
BEHIND THE PROBLEM, BUT WHAT CAN WE DO
TO HELP CHANGE TWITCH'S BEHAVIOR?

Here are some important points to remember...

Keep in mind that Twitch is usually very sweet and loving; he's not always angry. Furthermore, it's not his anger per se that causes him so much trouble, but rather his inability to self-regulate his emotions and handle frustration. There are three ways we can help:

1. By making use of activities to help build children's emotional awareness and self-control

2. By adopting activities and strategies parents/educators can use to manage out-of-control anger

3. By making use of charts and reward strategies that reinforce a child's newly found emotional awareness and self-control

Activities to Build Emotional Awareness & Self-Control

Throughout the activities I will recommend which "Twitch" is best for each activity. Below is a quick reminder chart you can refer to if you needed. For the full description of each "Twitch" personality, go to page 10.

HT
Hyper Reactive Twitch

ET
Entitled Twitch

IT
Irritable Twitch

ST
Self-Focused Twitch

VT
Volcanic Twitch

OT
Oppositional Twitch

1. Book Therapy (Bibliotherapy)
Ages 2–10 years

Good stories for children can really engage them as they identify with the characters and their feelings. We are going to use Andi Green's book, *The Very Frustrated Monster*, as the basis for our exercise. After reading the book to your child, have a chat along the following lines:

1. "Tell me how you think Twitch was feeling after he saw his bread had been snatched by a mouse? Do you think he was feeling calm or angry, sad or happy, frustrated or relaxed?"

2. "What other things upset Twitch?" In the story, his alarm didn't ring, he stubbed his toe, he knocked over his backpack, and he bumped his head. See how many things your child can recall.

3. "Who caused these problems?" Hopefully, your child will get the idea that each problem was no one's fault and just an accident. Your child might even get the idea that Twitch didn't check that his alarm was switched on and that got him off to a bad start. If kids understand this concept, they're well on the way to shifting from an unhealthy outlook to a more healthy "in-look."

4. "Why did Twitch yell at his friends?" "What was he like on the bus?" "Was he still upset and carrying his anger all the way to school?"

5. "Do you think yelling at his friends was fair?"

6. "Do you feel sorry for Twitch?"

7. Have you ever felt like Twitch did?" "Can you think of what things made you feel like that?"

8. "What lessons did Twitch learn from the squirrel?" You can help your child find answers: when things are not going right, just remember that it's a part of life; some things go right, some don't. The message we are trying to get across is that it's not what happens to us but how we handle it that has an effect on our lives.

9. "What else could Twitch have done to beat his frustration?" Your child may come up with ideas such as Twitch talked to his mom, used his belly or "volcano" breathing (see below), or dealt with the pesky Put-Down Bug (see below) who made him feel worthless.

10. "What do you think Twitch should do the next time he feels confused or frustrated?" This is a summary question to round out the discussion and provide a way forward.

2. Beating the Put-Down Bug Game
Ages 2–10 years

Renee, one of my 8-year-old clients, was very down on herself and couldn't enjoy anything in her life. In an attempt to deal with her problem, I decided to use as my therapeutic weapon, The WorryBug plush toy, from Andi Green's *Don't Feed the WorryBug*. I gave it to Renee to cuddle and then asked her to tell me about the creature she was holding. She grinned and said it was a cute little doll that had two big eyes. She loved its purple color, and she loved cuddling it.

When I explained to her that this cute little thing was actually making her life miserable, she looked at me in surprise! "Yes," I said. "This is the Put-Down Bug that keeps telling you that you're useless, that kids think you're dumb and stupid." I asked her if its voice said anything else bad about her. Renee then told me all the terrible things it said. "OK," I replied. "What if we put an end to letting it control your life? I'm going to give you some tricky ways to make it stop its silly behavior! And when you and your mom tell me that you've beaten the Put-Down Bug, I'm going to let you keep it! This will help you remember that it's just a cute little plush toy and that you will never again let it boss you around."

Renee took that on as a challenge. Mom and Renee and I talked about what she would do if the Put-Down Bug started to boss her around and make her feel bad (see discussion questions on pg 21). After that, I told her all about The Mind Muscle Victory Chart. I explained that this was like a game. Each time she was tempted to let her frustrations get the best of her, she should do something positive to calm herself down. If she succeeded, I asked her to jot it down on the MMV Chart (appendix - pg II). From then on, each time we met, she would look longingly at the Put-Down Bug on the shelf and tell me how many points she had thus far. Not long ago, Renee and her mom both said that the bug was not her boss anymore, and I kept my promise. Out the door they went, big grins on their faces, with this simple little Put-Down Bug clutched in Renee's arms. As the Put-Down Bug disappeared, I thought I detected just a hint on its googly eyed face that it was happy just being Renee's friend! Maybe I've been working too long with kids.

If you'd like to try this approach with your child, here's a general format. Using the book *The Very Frustrated Monster* as your starter, ask the child questions as outlined for Activity One. But this time, when he blames himself, not others, continue with a simple explanation and discussion of the Put-Down Bug as outlined here.

Discussion:

• "Did you know that many kids and grown-ups have inner thoughts that blame them and make them feel bad? Let's call that inner voice the Put-Down Bug. You may also want to introduce the WorryBug as the little culprit here. He is happiest when he's making you feel sad. Maybe he tells you you're 'silly' or 'stupid.'"

• "What words does your Put-Down Bug say to/about you?"

• "Do you think Twitch got angry because he really felt he was 'silly and stupid'?"

• "Do you ever hear thoughts in your head, putting you down?"

• "When was the last time that happened?"

• Parent: Try to think of a recent time when your child got very angry with herself over some little accident and discuss that incident. Children are much better at getting involved when the situation discussed has recently affected them.

• "Next time the Put-Down Bug gives you a hard time, what will we say back to him?" (See what response your child would like, such as "Bug off and get out of my life," or "Get lost, Put-Down Bug," or "I'm running my life, and I'm not listening to you anymore—everybody makes mistakes").

Put-Down Bug extension activity for parents and children:
If a parent has a similar problem (e.g., always putting himself/herself down), then a good extension to this child-focused exercise is for the parent to ask the child to help find more positive ways to deal with the adult's Put-Down Bug thoughts. In other words, the roles are reversed, and the child helps the parent; it's very empowering for children to think that they can not only help themselves, but can help others too.

3. Reading the Signals Activity
Ages 3–6 years

Directions:

Steps 1
Trace around a coin on a sheet of paper to create six circles or use the prepared ones below. Draw a different feeling on each face: happy, sad, surprised, afraid, disgusted, and angry.

Step 2
Ask your Twitch to make up his own facial expressions to show each of those feelings. Maybe you have to guess which feeling he is trying to show. Alternatively, you can make your own facial expressions for all six, and your child has to guess which ones you're showing.

Step 3
Chat about what sort of things make him feel like the emotion you're referring to (i.e., what makes him feel happy, angry, sad, afraid, etc.).

happy   sad   surprised

afraid   disgusted   angry

Step 4

Return to the book *The Very Frustrated Monster* and see if your child can identify those things that made Twitch feel angry, frustrated, or sad.

Step 5

Next, shift the focus away from those negative emotions and see if he can identify positive feelings (e.g., happy, calm, brave, surprised, friendly).

Step 6

Then, try to pinpoint things in your child's life that bring on those good feelings.

Step 7

Combining the above steps, see which of those things he would like to do to help him feel better when he's feeling hurt, frustrated, angry, or afraid. Feel free to add a few ideas, such as doing his breathing exercise (mentioned below), walking away from a situation, or telling his mom or the caregiver how he's feeling. Other options to help him feel better could include having some safe outlet to get rid of the frustration, such as beating up a pillow, jumping on a trampoline, bouncing a ball, playing with the dog, going on a swing, or just playing with water.

Step 8

By way of follow-up, in the evening, see if your child can recall times when he started to feel bad or the Put-Down Bug attacked. Did he manage to beat it; how did he do it?

AN ALTERNATIVE BUT LESS THREATENING APPROACH FOR "SELF-FOCUSED" Twitch (ST)
Some kids often find it easier to learn about emotional management via on-screen activities, rather than face-to-face confrontations with people. Non-human or machine characters, such as Thomas the Tank Engine or The WorryWoos Monsters, offer less threatening alternatives for emotional learning for ST children. One little boy I was dealing with was obsessed with Thomas, so his mom knitted and stuffed a Thomas for him. Young Paul would carry it around with him to feel safe and secure; when he got upset, he would just hug Thomas to help himself calm down.

A Cambridge University program has capitalized very effectively on this style using Transporters (www.TheTransporters.com). Faces on the machines, rather than on people, reflect the emotions, and the ST-style child often seems to learn more about feelings this way. Certainly, the Cambridge program is claiming big gains through this approach.

4. Reflecting the Blame Game
Ages 4–8 years

If your child blames everyone for everything, an activity that invites conversation and dialog is a good activity for kids of school readiness age or older. Should your Twitch begin to rail and rave against someone, gently begin an investigative conversation to determine the facts. You could say:

- "I know that you're very sad and that you're angry with X, but let's do detective work. Why don't we write down (or draw or talk about) all the things that happened." When you have finished, proceed to the next step to open up discussion.

- "Now I know that X did things that annoyed you. But, so we're fair, let's also talk about anything you did that may have annoyed him." You may even use two of the WorryWoos plush toys to role play the incident, pausing along the way to ask, "How did Twitch/you feel?" Then ask, "How do you think … (the other plush toy) felt?"

"This self-awareness is an important and vital social skill."

If young Twitch has enough awareness to see that his own actions may have played a part in the crisis, then that's great news. It means he can make changes in his game plan, take some responsibility, and start to handle setbacks better. However, keep in mind that kids may not be able to beat the blame game if parents can't—that is, if parents are big on blaming someone else, kids will copy.

5. Beating the Cranky Bug Game
Ages 2–8 years

This activity is similar to Beating the Put-Down Bug (No. 2) but geared to more aggressive behavior. Again, the WorryWoos WorryBug can be used, but this time labelled as the Cranky Bug. Explore when the Cranky Bug starts to take over.

- "What feelings do you get when the Cranky Bug is gaining power?"

- "When does it attack?"

- "What does it tell you to do (e.g., yell, push, hit, scream, be rude, swear)?"

- "What will you do the next time he attacks?"

- Review options, like speaking in a calm voice, using volcano or belly breathing, or being a "cool" kid.

- "How can we record our mind muscle victories over the Cranky Bug?"

Additional Comments
Use the Mind Muscle Victory Chart, referred to in Activity No. 2, to record how your Twitch is doing. If Twitch is into iPads or equivalent technology, check out an app that charts progress (see www.bestappsforkids.com for some examples). Just remember that we're rewarding kids for mind muscle victories when they've shown that they are able to stay in control and beat the Cranky Bug. If you feel your child isn't trying to change the game plan, then you will need to apply consequences to move him on. The use of consequences is explained in more detail in the next section.

6. Squeeze the Ball Activity
Ages 5–8 years

You've probably worked out that what we're trying to achieve with these breathing and squeezing activities is to put some space between an angry FEELING and angry RESPONSE. It's a bit like the old counting-to-10 technique. Unfortunately, some kids count to 10 superfast, and they're still angry! This Squeeze the Ball Activity adds a bit more imagination and flair.

Directions:

- Find some little ball that fits comfortably into the child's pocket (e.g., a commercial stress ball or squash ball).

- When she's angry, encourage her to squeeze the ball and keep squeezing until the muscles in her forearms get tired.

- This experience of feeling arm tiredness means that the mind muscle has won the day! Boys often like this challenge, especially if you can give big cheers when the mind muscle has won. Don't forget to record her progress on the Mind Muscle Victory Chart (see page 43 for more information on making a chart).

- Say something along these lines: "Well done; you're becoming a real tough nut."

- You may want tell the child that, if she doesn't have a ball with her at the time she gets angry, she can make a fist and squeeze hard until the arm muscle gets tired. (Some therapists use the image of a tube of toothpaste, instead of a ball; kids visualize squeezing the tube and the pent-up anger snaking out of it.)

7. Bubble Breathing Activity
Ages 2–11 years

Staying in control of our emotions is really all about breath control. *The Very Frustrated Monster* tells us that Twitch tried it when he counted to 10, but that was neither long enough nor clever enough. In bubble breathing, we're trying to give kids an actual physical aid (or its image) to help them slow down their breathing, regain self-control, and relax. One way is for children to pretend, or actually have, a drink in a cup with a straw in it. They then breathe in through the nose and then gently breathe out through the mouth using the straw to make bubbles in the drink. Breathing must be controlled—soft and slow—so nothing spills. Let your child know that it may take up to 20 slow breaths before he feels calmer.

- One young boy I was treating really liked the idea of the bubble after reading about the character Squeek in *The Monster in the Bubble*. This young fellow had not retreated into his bubble as Squeek had done but was a very angry little boy. What he decided to do was use his breathing to create a big safe bubble all around himself where things didn't frustrate him and he could calm down. When he felt OK again, he would just "walk out of his bubble" to the applause of his family.

- A variation on this bubble creation is to get the over-reactive child (especially HT) to take slow, deep breaths to create a bubble and imagine floating off inside that bubble, away from frustrations to some imagined site, like the beach, a farm, or other favorite place where things are more relaxed and calming.

- A neat meditational variation on this bubble technique for children in the 7- to 11-year-old group (also available for older children and adults) is included in the free app "Smiling Mind." Simply go to the app icon on your cellphone or tablet, download the "Smiling Mind" app, and choose the appropriate age group. For the 7- to 11-year-old category, several breathing exercises are included. In the Bubble Journey, for instance, the child lies on the floor and inhales an imaginary colorful bubble into the belly. Next, she breathes out and sends the bubble down to her toes, letting it relax the toes. Then it floats up to her ankles and relaxes that part—then the calves, the knees, and so on until the bubble has visited, warmed, and relaxed each part of the child's tense little body.

I should add that you will have great trouble getting ET-style Twitches to even try bubble breathing and self-control: They expect others will solve problems for them.

8. Volcano Breathing Activity
Ages 5–10 years

Sometimes I adapt ideas from the useful program *A Volcano in My Tummy: Helping Children to Handle Anger* by Eliane Whitehouse and Warwick Pudney. I ask the children to imagine or draw the volcano. Instead of having it erupt in anger, they breathe up some hot, red volcanic lava, imagine spewing it down the side of the volcano, and watch it crash into the trees below. They repeat the process and breathe up more red lava until there is no more lava left. Not only do many kids like the imagery, but the exercise forces them to slow their breathing, take deeper breaths, and regain self-control.

Some programs in anger management refer to this boil over as the amygdala hijack. It means that when kids lose self-control, the amygdala or emotional center in the brain stem hijacks the brain and takes over.

9. Rainbow Breathing Activity
Ages 4–10 years

I love this story. Recently, I was dealing with an 8-year-old girl who had to cope with many horrific family issues. I had shown Grace volcano breathing but she said it was a "boy thing"! What Grace invented was rainbow breathing! She loved colorful rainbows, and yellow and green were her favorite colors. Her creative idea was to imagine a rainbow; when she was angry, the purple and red colors were on top. She would breathe out over the arc of the rainbow and take the angry colors down to the bottom of the rainbow. Then, she would try to pull up the yellow and green colors; she would keep trying until her favorite colors appeared at the top of the rainbow, giving her peace. How clever is this little champion!

Recommend for: HT, IT, VT, ET, ST, OT

10. Belly Breathing
(for all ages)

"Belly breathing" is a popular exercise done in many school classes as part of a daily relaxation routine. The children are asked to lie down, put their hands on their bellies, and feel the rise and fall as they breathe in and out. Then they're encouraged to slow it down and deliberately push the belly out (diaphragm breathing) as they breathe in and gently flatten the belly as they breathe out. Often, this action is combined with sending the breath down to each part of the body in turn to relax it. Kids love doing this class exercise, and it's often combined with meditation, which young kids really enjoy.

11. The Shaker Jar

Finding strategies that put some time between the frustration and the angry response is critical. Young Max taught me one that worked for him. Max's dad cleaned up a plastic peanut spread jar, took off the label, renamed it "Shaker Jar," filled it with water, and then added some of those snowflakes that are used in the Christmas decorations called "snow globes." When Max could feel himself getting angry, he would go to his jar and shake it again and again and then do slow breathing to help the flakes settle to the bottom. (Parents, of course, could use any safe ingredient that just took a bit of time to settle.) It really worked for Max.

Postscript: All of these resources do have their limitations. Unfortunately, Max was in trouble again at school the other day for hitting another boy. It turned out that this boy had run off with his Shaker Jar, and that was too much for Max!

12. Other Breathing Exercises

There are many other breathing exercises. One that my colleague uses, as part of relaxation, is a candle. Kids (or adults) look at it for a minute and then look away with eyes shut and watch the black and red after image. When it fades, they repeat the process, blocking out all other thoughts. It's marvelous for the blood pressure! His variation is that children have to then blow on the candle without blowing it out—in other words, exhale with soft and gentle breaths.

13. Massage
Ages 2–8 years, but good for any age

Have you noticed that many of the uptight and angry kids are "cuddle shy"? We all benefit from skin touch to earth or ground our tension, or what I term "earthing" our "emotional electricity." That cuddly contact helps us to relax and defuse angry feelings.

Some kids are just not cuddly from day one; others you can only soften after the bath or some other skin-soothing experience. The techniques below can be very useful but are best done in a calm environment where you're calm and your child feels the same way—maybe just before bed and perhaps with the help of some essential oils, such as a calming mix. Anyhow, here are two fun ways that were referred to in my other book *Helping Young Worriers Beat the WorryBug*.

Car Wash Method

Directions: Have the child lie on her back with eyes closed. Gently hold each arm and pretend she is going through a car wash.

- Rinse Cycle - **Gently run your fingers from her shoulders to her fingers.**
- Wash Cycle - **Gently massage the arm like the soft car wash brushes.**
  - The Rag Wash - **Tickle her arm with a soft rag or cloth.**
  - Final Rinse - **Run your fingers up and down each arm.**
  - Blow Dry - **Blow gently on each arm.**

FRUSTRATION FREE CAR WASH

Weather Report Method

Directions: Have the child lie on his tummy with eyes closed. Talk about the weather report that he's seen on the TV and explain that you're going to do a weather report on his body. It's easy for the parent to learn, feels good to the child, and is one weather report that can accurately forecast a cool change!

Snowflakes
Tap fingers rapidly and lightly on the child's head, shoulders, and back.

Raindrops
Do the same as for snowflakes but a little harder.

Thunderclaps
Cup your hands and clap them across the back and shoulders.

Tornado
Place your hands on the child's shoulders and circle your thumbs down either side of the spine and across the shoulders.

Tidal wave
Slide your hands up and down the arms and across the back.

Calm after the storm
Rest your hands on, then above, his shoulders for a few moments.

14. Coloring-in Activity (for adults and children)

Who would have believed that the simple act of coloring-in turns out to be so effective in helping adults soothe stress and slow busy brainwaves. There are many explanations for this phenomenon, which I won't go into here. Suffice it to say that, if parents have (buy or download) some coloring-in sheets for adults, then using them with their kids not only helps relieve their own tensions but may also be an enjoyable and useful activity for their children.

15. Environmental Activity
(for all types and all ages, including parents)

Have you noticed that children's behavior is dramatically affected by the environment they're in… great at grandma's, horrible at home, saintly at school, cranky in the car, etc.? The softer the environment, the more likely it is to produce calmer behavior in the child.

- Play softer calming music, like nature sounds or semi-classical music, as background at home.
- At home, burn essential aromatic oils that induce calmer thinking (neroli, sandalwood, chamomile, lavender) or just buy a calming mix.
- Have regular quiet and "screen-less" time in your child's daily routine. Desirable activities include drawing, crafts, reading, and using Play-Doh® or a sand tray. This quiet time could be used to just download your child's day and chat about any issues that may have bothered her.
- In a group setting, set up a fish tank where uptight kids can sit and sense the calmness of the fish and the white noise of the bubbles.
- Use water. A bubble bath or a shower can soothe the skin, particularly in sensory sensitive kids. Consider running a small indoor fountain or waterfall.
- In a group setting, get a small pet—like a hamster or hermit crab—that the kids can watch and learn to care for. But don't believe their promises that they will do all the caring forever—I've yet to see it!

The previous 15 activities, all aimed at helping kids build their emotional awareness and self-control, are at least a good start. Don't try them all. Choose or adapt ones that appeal to you. If you've created a good one, I'd be keen to hear about it. Let us know at WorryWoos.com/DrJohn.html.

Now let's move on to the more difficult task of finding ways to manage anger and aggression.

ACTIVITIES AND STRATEGIES FOR PARENTS/EDUCATORS TO MANAGE ANGER AND AGGRESSION

You've probably noticed that nearly all healthy 2-year-olds will resort to the biff (i.e., sharp blow with the fist) and bite when they're frustrated. That's normal; the ego has just "arrived." They think that the world revolves around them and that they should get whatever they want! In time and with loving care, they learn how to share and cope with frustration. In fact, we all have to learn to handle our frustrations and anger without hurting others, ourselves, or things that surround us.

I would like every home in the universe to have the motto "violence by either adults or children in the family home is NEVER OK." Unfortunately, anger is not an easy urge to control, so here are some suggestions:

- Self-control strategy – It's absolutely essential that, as the adult, you stay in control of your own anger. If you feel your temperature rising, then that's the time to start your deep breathing, so your mind stays on top of the mayhem.

- Parental time-out strategy – If you're angry, that's dangerous. If your angry child is safe, take your own TIME OUT. Remove yourself from the scene and go somewhere quiet or go outdoors. Get your breathing under control and don't return to the situation until your mind is clear enough to take control.

- Do nothing strategy – If the child is having a harmless little tantrum, then it's often best to just let the situation play itself out. Once kids reach the age of about 18–24 months, they crave to become independent. They know what they want but all too often lack the skills to be able to do it. The result is… the tantrum.

- Playful strategy – I've had some bizarre playful suggestions from parents on how to handle tantrums—from holding a mirror up in front of the child so he stops to watch to a parent's getting down on the floor and acting out a bigger tantrum. One grandma did just that in the supermarket. The 4-year-old stopped his tantrum, just stared at her, and then whispered, "Grandma, stop it. Get up, get up." It worked for her! Because shopping centers are prime spots for tantrums, one dad made up a sign that read "TANTRUM IN PROGRESS; DO NOT DISTURB" and put it on the side of the shopping cart so other parents would understand.

- In general, these performances die down with time and age, so don't take them too seriously. It's hard work being 2! Empathize with your child—solve the problem together. Get down to the child's eye level and use words such as "Sounds like you're having a hard time today; can I help you in any way?" Chances are that a calm attitude like this will halve the duration and intensity of the performance.

- The calming hug strategy – If YOU are OK, but your toddler is out of control and angry, then you may need to just encircle her with your arms. Cuddle your child and whisper or just gently sway to take the edge off her anger. This bodily contact grounds her tension, or what I term "emotional electricity," and makes a child feel more secure.

- Safety embrace – When the behavior is dangerous or destructive, I've sometimes recommended using the safety embrace (for toddlers and children up to 4 years).

  - The parent moves behind the child and holds him in a cross-over seat belt style grip (with both arms crossed) to hold the child's opposite arm.

  - Then the parent slides down to his knees bringing the child gently down in front of him to sit, so that the child's legs are stretched out horizontally in front. In this position, the child can't kick or head butt the parent.

  - The parent should hold the child firmly and whisper gentle words or even sing lullabies or favorite songs, until the child shows signs of calming down and regaining some self-control. Parents should use this technique only if they're calm and only with younger children.

  - This technique is not to be used on children who have been traumatized or abused and must only be done under professional advice. Always end the safety embrace with a positive little calming or cuddling activity together. Problem solving about the anger episode will have to wait until things are much calmer.

Traffic Light Strategy (for school-age children)

This is a slight variation on the time-out method but has a little more form to it. Discuss traffic lights, how they work, and what each color means. GREEN means keep going, AMBER or YELLOW lights warn that danger may lie ahead, and RED means stop.

- Ask your child if he knows what "red lights"—dangerous feelings or behaviors—he has to control or stop.

- Talk about developing some YELLOW-LIGHT activities to help him shift his behavior back from angry red behavior to happy, green-light territory. Here's how to develop this YELLOW-LIGHT activity:

- If he can't calm down or isn't trying, then point out that he has hit the RED LIGHT. Send him to his room or designated quiet corner as a time out to cool off. There you can make use of YELLOW-LIGHT ideas (above) that encourage more acceptable behavior

    - Get a sheet of yellow cardboard.
    - Trace around a dinner plate or object of similar size.
    - On the yellow circle, write or draw (depending on the child's age) cool things the child can decide to do when he comes out of the time-out are. Cool or acceptable activities could include playing with the dog or with blocks to using the iPhone, watching TV, helping mom, reading a book, or playing with toys.
    - Cut the circle out and affix it to the wall in the time-out area.

- Explain to your Twitch that he will be heading for a RED LIGHT when he breaks a house rule or starts to get agitated, but doesn't attempt to slow down or change his behavior.

- If your child won't go to the time-out area, then (per time-out notes above), FIRMLY take him—without hitting or aggression—to that time-out place. On the way, remind him of which house rule was broken so that he knows why there's a penalty.

- When he has calmed down and picked a YELLOW-LIGHT activity, then he can ask to come out and pursue that activity. If you think he is ready and has chosen a good activity, you may then give him the GREEN LIGHT to do so.

- Many parents set a time limit for time out and use an oven timer or similar device to indicate when the time is up. As mentioned above, generally the rule of thumb is 1 minute per year of age (e.g., 2 minutes plus up to 10 minutes maximum for an older child).

- If, after your child has completed the activity, his anger is still too hot to handle, then it's back to his time-out area to choose a stronger or better (YELLOW LIGHT) activity.

- If he can't calm down or isn't trying, then point out that he has hit the RED LIGHT. Send him to his room or designated quiet corner as a time out to cool off. There you can make use of YELLOW-LIGHT ideas (above) that encourage more acceptable behavior.

- After a time out, talk about why he got into trouble, what was bugging him, and what he could do if he feels that way again. He may even want your advice on how you would handle the same situation.

- The goal is to reach some clear and mutually agreed-upon plan for the future

- If the situation does not improve despite promises and apologies, then consult a child or clinical psychologist with a reputation for success in behavior management.

For younger children, (ages 2½ to 5 years), here is a slight variation on the above:

Although children 3 years and older typically know their colors, many in this age group have little or no insight into the cause of problem behaviors. Here's a more basic version for those children. The parent

1. RED=STOP
   Note certain behaviors (e.g., shouting or hitting) that are out of control.
   Tell your child to go to the time-out spot—a quiet corner or bedroom will do—to think about the problem behavior.

2. YELLOW=BE CAREFUL
   Think about ideas and activities the child can do later (as above); draw pictures of such activities on the yellow cardboard circle.

3. GREEN=GO
   Give the child permission to continue when a good activity has been selected after time out.

Your child will learn to stay in the time-out place for about 1–3 minutes or until the timer trips. When time is up, remind her of which rule was broken. You may also want to talk about what she can do the next time she feels angry. This might include getting a cuddle from mom or telling someone what is upsetting her. There's nothing wrong with a good old howl! But try concentrating on her good points, and you'll get much better behavior. Kids tend to play up to or down to our expectations, as reflected in the labels we use. Now let's look at ways to reward and correct your child's behavior..

Using Positive Rewards

We all love being rewarded, but kids are fanatical about it. If we can reward behavior we like with praise, privileges, points, or freedoms, that's always our first and preferred option. For rewards to work, there are a few elements that need to be recognized.

1. Novelty is usually important: new stickers, a new chart, or a new app all help the child stay motivated to achieve the goal. If the same reward has been used for weeks, it won't have any pulling power.

2. The reward has to be more exciting than the child's usual routine. Having a trip to get ice cream won't be motivating if she gets ice cream every day!

3. The reward has to be earned. If she hasn't achieved a step toward the behavior goal, then don't give in to her pester power.

4. Having said that, make the reward achievable and not vague—don't reward her simply for "being good." The behavior must be specific and short-term (e.g., an instance of showing self-control or mind muscle control).

5. Rewards and incentives won't stay motivating unless parents put in effort and enthusiasm. If you're not excited about her progress and rewards then your child won't be either.

6. But sometimes all the positives aren't enough to bring about change, and we have to invoke negative consequences.

Punishment is something I rarely use. It's something we inflict on kids "to teach them a lesson." For instance, we might smack a child for poking his sister as he walked past. There are three problems with this style. First, the kids are likely to copy and become smackers. The second problem is that it doesn't teach them what to do—just what not to do. The third problem is that the smack is meant to hurt, and kids are more likely to respond by contemplating revenge, rather than expressing remorse.

Consequences, by contrast, are natural or logical outcomes of the children's own actions. For instance, in the poking-sister example, the parent could acknowledge that the offender has trouble walking past his sister without poking her. Then, as that behavior seems hard for him to change, the parent will give him some practice in walking past his sister, as many times as needed, without poking her, until he can do it every time. If the behavior re-emerges, then they would do more practice. In other words, the remedial strategy is a direct and logical consequence of the child's own actions. Once he has learned the behavior, reward that better behavior with hugs, cuddles, points, or a celebration of some sort. To make sure your negative consequences are healthy and helpful, they must meet these conditions:

1. Don't use physical punishment.

2. Work with your child (if the child is 4 years old or older) to address the problem behavior.

3. Make sure training the new behavior is logical (i.e., related to the problem behavior).

4. End the training or practice session the same day if possible.

5. Be consistent when correcting bad behavior using these exercises (i.e., mom, dad, and grandparents should all use similar standards/criteria).

6. Keep the goal in mind: Get back to positives as quickly as possible.

Older children (7+ years) will not do (nor do they need) the practice component above. The parent and child can discuss and together determine penalties or rewards the child will receive based on the child's specific actions.

The best way to cement or reward desired behavior varies with age.

- With toddlers and children under 3,
  the best way to affirm good behavior and self-control is just the good old hug, cuddle, smile, and other such expressions of approval.

- With 3- to 4-year-olds,
  the old cuddle is still a potent reward but symbolic rewards, such as stickers and very simple charts, also work well. For instance, a good one is to first draw a big round dinner plate circle on the fridge with a marker pen; that's the face outline. Then, as the child shows some behavior that you want to reward, put one feature on the face with a whiteboard pen. For a 3-year-old, we might start with three features (eyes and nose). When the child completes the chart (wins a smiling mouth), he gets a reward. That reward could be something simple, like a favorite meal, special game, or play date with a friend. Then rub off the facial features and start again. As the child gets older you can add more features (e.g., ears and hair tufts) before he gets the smiley mouth. Feel free to make up your own simple incentive games that would work with your child.

- For 4- to 9-year-olds,
  we can use more elaborate charts. Remember that the aim is to reward the specific desired behavior, not reward the child just for being "good."

As we're trying to build self-control, here's a Mind Muscle Victory Chart you may be able to use. For instance, if your Twitch has often said that he's stupid, but begins to shift toward using more positive language (e.g., "It was just an accident" or "I'm not stupid; everyone makes mistakes"), record specific victories he achieves as he builds a record of success in changing his behavior. These entries can be cumulative (per the example below from one of my clinical cases) or take the form of a success ladder that orders behaviors in terms of their difficulty or significance in reaching the goal.

Mind Muscle Victory Chart

10. Played nicely when his friends came over

9. Stayed in control when mom didn't buy him a yo-yo

8. Used his shaker jar to stay calm when he was upset

7. Gave mom a big hug to help him feel better

6. Stayed calm when he told the teacher that kids were being mean to him

5. Put on his favorite music when he was getting upset

4. Went to his room quietly when he was upset

3. Helped mom to stay calm when she was upset

2. Colored pictures to keep calm

1. Did homework calmly

For children over the age of 9, these visual aids aren't needed or wanted. Children can now keep their own records of success and their rewards will be in their own sense of better control, becoming more popular, and feeling happier.

Now it's time to reflect.

- Do you feel you understand your Twitch better?
- If you reassess your child's symptoms on the 0-to-2 scale profiled under each style (see pg 8-9), do you see some downgrading (e.g., from 2 to 1 or 1 to 0)?
- Can you recognize any of your own management style changes that may have helped make a difference?
- Which activities have you found useful and need to store in your mindset for future use?
- Can you recognize any of the following 10 best environmental factors that now operate at your place?

TOP 10 DOMESTIC ENVIRONMENT SUPPORTS TO HELP SELF-CONTROL

1. Parent is modelling calm, connected interactions within the family and wider community.

2. Parent(s) has developed a more cohesive, consistent, and predictable style of child management.

3. Sibling(s) may be treated differently but there is no favoritism in head, heart, or action.

4. The child/children have a healthy diet.

5. Less than 2 hours per day is spent by children on screen entertainment.

6. Parent(s) has modified a busy schedule to make life less hectic for the family and has included routine play, down time, meditation, relaxation, and talk time.

7. Parent(s) has made a distinct effort not to bring marital warfare into the life of the child/children.

8. Parent(s) is able to self-regulate emotions and anger.

9. Parent(s) uses positive management and consequences approach rather than negative management with physical punishment.

10. The child/children feel safe at home and at school.

FRUSTRATION WORK SHEET - PART 1

Directions: Make a list of what made you frustrated during the week. Then rate each frustration from 1 to 10—big outbursts are given high scores, and little occurrence are given low scores. On the Mind Muscle Victory Chart, record your victories on how you overcame each of these frustrations.

Frustration List	Date	Rating

Mind Muscle Victory Chart

1.

2.

3.

4.

5.

6.

7.

8.

9.

10.

DRAW YOUR CRANKY BUG

DRAW YOUR PUT-DOWN BUG

DRAW YOUR FRUSTRATION MONSTER

Frustration Notes

I hope that the book has been useful to you. Maybe you've created your own activities. If so, I would love to hear about them. Maybe they can be incorporated in the next edition. If you're not making the progress you need, then make an appointment with a clinical child psychologist. There may be other deep-seated factors that are making change hard to win.

Certainly, bringing up perfect kids from our own imperfect gene pool in a very imperfect and chaotic world has never been harder. Thank you for the perfectly imperfect job you are doing with love and laughter and with all the trials, triumphs, and tribulations that are part and parcel of our job as parents and teachers. Although the world may not recognize your contribution publicly, know that you are protecting the world's greatest resource: its children. I salute you and wish you well.

Available WorryWoo books and Dr. John companion books.

Emotion topic:	WorryWoo Book/Character	Companion Books by Dr. John
Anxiety, depression	*Don't Feed the WorryBug* (Wince)	*Helping Young Worriers Beat the WorryBug*
Frustration, anger	*The Very Frustrated Monster* (Twitch)	*Helping Young Children Manage Anger and Frustration*

Emotion topic:	WorryWoo Book/Character
Loneliness, rejection	*The Lonely Little Monster* (Nola)
Social confidence, shyness	*The Monster in the Bubble* (Squeek)
Body-image, self-esteem	*The Nose That Didn't Fit* (Rue)
Self confidence, assertion, bully management	*The Monster Who Couldn't Decide* (Fuddle)
Envy, jealousy, greed, bullying	*The Monster Who Wanted It All* (Zelly)

Resource:
Whitehouse, E., & Pudney, W. (1998). *A volcano in my tummy: helping children to handle anger—A resource book for parents, caregivers and teachers.* Gabriola Island, BC, Canada: New Society Publishers.